SCRAM

RELOCATING UNDER A NEW IDENTITY

SCRAM

RELOCATING UNDER A NEW IDENTITY

by
JAMES S. MARTIN
Attorney At Law

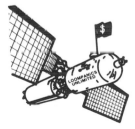

Loompanics Unlimited
Port Townsend, Washington

SCRAM: Relocating Under A New Identity
© 1993 by James S. Martin

Published by:
Loompanics Unlimited
PO Box 1197
Port Townsend, WA 98368
Loompanics is a division of Loompanics Enterprises, Inc.

Cover design by Steve O'Keefe

ISBN 1-55950-094-8
Library of Congress Catalog Card Number 93-78605

CONTENTS

ABOUT THE AUTHOR

After graduating from U.C. Berkeley, James S. Martin traveled around the world, including the South Pacific region. Settling in Australia for a period of five years, he obtained his first law degree from the University of New South Wales. He returned to California and obtained a second law degree from the McGeorge School of Law in Sacramento. During the following twelve years, he has practiced law in a small town on the coast of California and, during each of those years, has vacationed abroad. He teaches law at the Monterey College of Law and law-related subjects for the U.C. Extension Program.

INTRODUCTION

So you want to leave and start over somewhere new. Have you imagined a place where you would have a new residence, new friends, a new job, and a new identity? If so, I would not be surprised, because in my years of experience — several years traveling and living abroad, as well as several years of practicing law — I have met dozens of people who have planned or have actually created a "clean slate" of their lives. They were people who, for different reasons, created a new beginning by reinventing themselves.

Everyone eventually wants a break in their routines. Why else would we plan and pay for vacations? Most everyone feels fatigued with their careers and even their relationships. Why else would we consider job relocation to be an ordinary event and divorce the expected outcome of half of today's marriages? Like most attorneys, I have the type of practice where people call on me to be a problem-solver and I have become used to routines and careers being rearranged as solutions to problems. I have come to understand that it is common to wish for a new life.

Many forces keep us from a new beginning. There is the fear of the unknown. There is the paralyzing effect of debt — always an enemy to progress — that tells us we cannot "afford to go." The social system in which we live keeps us from leaving and the demise of any American frontier makes us believe that there is nowhere to go. Nevertheless, the boundaries of your life have as much to do with your imagination and courage as they have to do with the forces imposed upon you. The people that relocate under a new identity push against those forces and empower themselves.

I do not encourage or advise a new identity any more than I "command" a client to divorce, or file for bankruptcy, or litigate an issue. Those decisions are made by the adult clients — preferably, after much thought and consideration. What I can do, however, is to discuss the pros and cons of those decisions, then provide a cost-benefit analysis to my client. The attorney is merely a conduit for information, while the decisions are made by the client.

Along those lines, this book takes the form of a consultation with an adult individual who imagines or is actually effecting a radical change in his or her life by changing identity and residence location. It reads as a question-and-answer dialogue — much the same as an attorney-client interview would proceed. Ten chapters each consider one topic. Following each chapter is a short biographical sketch, or case history, which illustrates the content of the preceding chapter. The names of most of the individuals are fictitious, but the case histories are based on actual people and events.

Having said that any decision to relocate under a new identity is made by the reader, I make another intent clear: Nothing herein should be construed as instruction on how to break the law, nor should it be read as encouragement to do so. In fact, all of the information provided is intended to advise against breaking the law while the individual plans or effects a new identity.

Every day, the federal Justice Department creates new identities for criminals and the worst examples of society, as well as assisting them with taxpayer money! Why shouldn't that choice be available for other citizens? Why shouldn't you have the opportunity for a "clean slate?" If you do have the aim of reinventing yourself, be aware that you are not alone, nor were you the first to dream of it.

James S. Martin
Attorney at Law

CHAPTER ONE:
THE COMMITMENT
TO A NEW IDENTITY

1. Mental Preparation

2. Speed of the Change

3. Easing Out of Your Routines

4. Sharing Your Plans With a Friend

5. Assistance from Friends

6. Helping Yourself to Decide

7. Change May Be Scary

8. Right and Wrong Reasons to Change

1. **How is mental preparation part of assuming a new identity?**

    Be honest with yourself when you consider relocation under a new identity. Do you have what it takes?

    There will be the loss of all friends and family, together with changes in your employment and social routines all the way from your favorite local bar to your favorite local church. On the other hand, those very things may be the sources of your desire to relocate, so they may be encouragement to leave.

    A new location and a new identity can be either thrilling or troubling. The difference depends on your mental state.

2. **Should the change be quick or gradual?**

    For reasons that will be explained as you read this book, relocation under a new identity would be most successful when accomplished quickly, but after careful and discreet preparations.

3. **Why couldn't I "ease out" of relationships and routines?**

    Do you want to stay with the status quo, or do you want a new life and a new identity? Your instinct to hang on to the old you is a signal that you are reluctant to change. If so, maybe you should stay who and where you are.

4. **Why can't I tell someone I plan to start over? All I want is the support of a trusted person. What's wrong with that?**

    Firstly, think about why you would need validation or encouragement from a family member or a friend. Are you so deeply interwoven into those patterns that you cannot leave? Would you rather talk about the adventure of relocating under a new identity or actually do that? Your desire to involve even one trusted person shows that your commitment is not complete.

Secondly, interviews at your last place of employment and/or hangouts are often done as part of missing persons searches. The sharing of your plans and preparations — even showing someone this book — is a security breach. Rule Number One is to make up your mind about relocation under a new identity, then shut up about it.

5. Won't I need some assistance?

Probably not. Delegating any part of your plan would be a mistake for the reasons discussed above. This is such an important, fundamental issue that it bears repeating: A genuine commitment to a new identity is a *private* decision about a radical change of life. If you need support from your best pal, Billy Joe, or if you are mooning over leaving your girlfriend and need to let her down easy, you haven't got what it takes to start over with a new life.

As far as physical assistance in effecting your "getaway," everything can (and should) be accomplished by you. Catch a cab to the airport rather than asking a friend for a ride. Mail your own letters which will set up a false trail rather than trusting them to someone else.

6. How can I help myself decide whether I have the necessary commitment to a new identity?

Use an old learning technique: Write about it and visualize it. Make a list of benefits (potential help and assistance) which you will probably receive during the next few years. Will somebody bring you into their business? Will you inherit from Aunt Polly? Is employment booming in your area? Next, make a list of the problems from those same sources during that same time. Hassles from a girlfriend? So-called friends taking advantage of you? No market for your skills in that area?

Which list "weighs more?" Are you better off staying or leaving? Analyze the choice as a business decision, then let your choice be swift and certain. The choice cannot come from your minister, your best friend, or your lawyer. It is an absolutely private decision.

7. **I must admit that the commitment to a radical change in my life scares me.**

The tone of this book is meant to be non-coercive as well as recognizing your freedom to choose. I cannot force you to make any decision — indeed, I will not even recommend that a decision be made. If you do decide — whether it is a decision to relocate, or a decision to stay — that conclusion is your choice.

Choices are actions and actions take courage. Your candor about your fear shows some courage — the courage to admit that you are scared. Keep in mind that a brave man need not be fearless. Perhaps I can help you by saying that the anticipation of new events (first day of school, first ride on the chair lift to the top of the hill) is usually worse than the experience of sitting through those new classes or the thrill of skiing down the hill.

8. **Do you say that there are right and wrong reasons to assume a new identity?**

Despite some people abhorring value judgments, I must tell you that some reasons would definitely be wrong.

Abandonment of dependent children would be unconscionable; relocation to rid yourself of an ex-lover who is stalking you is understandable. Interstate flight to avoid criminal prosecution is a crime; beginning with a clean reputation in a new community is desirable.

Now, what are your reasons? Are they acceptable to your own code of ethics? Are they acceptable to society? If your decision is made for the right reasons, it will be easier to live with and you will not wrestle with regrets.

Case History:
Charlie, The Loser

Charlie left a small, midwestern town where all of his friends, and the police, thought of him as a clownish type with a weakness for pot. He did not finish high school and had worked in a series of dead-end jobs, always being the first to be laid off when times were slow. His last job had been night shift at a convenience store. He was fired when owner-ship changed hands.

"I suppose it was my fault, but nobody took me seriously," said Charlie. "I was seen as a drop out, a goof off, not to be trusted with anything but the lowest job." Charlie continued to tell me about how his reputation began in high school, how it compounded with an arrest for marijuana, and how it was like a monster from a horror movie — refusing to die no matter what he did.

"The cops could be friendly with most motorists. With me, it had to be an out-of-the-car pat down and a look into my car. I gave up pot after my one hassle, but to the cops and my friends' parents, I was a Bolivian druglord. I was discrimi-nated against in a way that some people do not understand."

Charlie's commitment was an easy step: He was single, his mom had passed away, and his father had left when Charlie was in grade school. His luck with women was dismal, so Charlie had no romantic attachments to his midwestern town.

"I sold the few things I owned, including my car, and that was my grubstake. I decided on a new name because — right or wrong — I was not going to pay bills before I left." When I asked Charlie about his goals, he had a quick reply. "I wanted a new reputation and I wanted a chance to work. Those things were not going to happen in my hometown."

The next decisions were good ones. He went to Las Vegas where there is a year-round tourist/gambling industry that does not require college education of its employees. Charlie was willing to work nights and he found a job. He did not need a car at first, finding Las Vegas a small town and the bus system convenient. He stayed clean and sober in a party town, was always on time for work, and soon had a reputation for, of all things, reliability.

Charlie laughs at the suggestion that relocation under a new identity was scary. "I was young and had the ability to start over without a 'loser' reputation. It was the best thing I could have done."

CHAPTER TWO:
SOCIAL REORGANIZATION

1. Social Changes Due to Relocation

2. Reasons for Divorce Before Relocation

3. The Business Part of Divorce

4. Divesting Personal Property

5. Default Dissolution

6. Relocation Involving Children

7. Financial Obligations and Relocation

8. Bankruptcy

9. Bankruptcy Process

10. Drawbacks of Bankruptcy

1. What changes will take place in my life?

Everything. You will be leaving family, friends, your job, familiar routines, and the geography you have become used to.

On the other hand, you may have few helpful family members, no loyal friends, no valuable career that could not be found elsewhere, a hankering to leave Detroit for the West, secret desires to keep going west and tend bar in Lahaina, Maui, and no aversion to hitching a ride on a yacht leaving Lahaina to drop in on a South Sea island.

Therefore, the changes may be losses or gains depending on your mindset. I hate to keep harping on the commitment to change, but it is a fundamental consideration for someone planning to relocate under a new identity.

2. Should I file for divorce before I leave?

That might not be a bad idea. The reasons for filing would include firming up your psychological commitment, "freeing" your partner, and taking care of the legal and business ends of that relationship.

3. What do you mean about the "business ends" of my marriage?

Most couples own property; if not real property, there would be personal property such as vehicles, household goods and appliances, kitchenware, and electronics. You will want to divide any property as well as settling obligations (your debts).

If you are going to sell items of personal property to finance your relocation, it would only be fair to sell your own property and not personal items which rightfully belong to your spouse. After all, if you leave having wrongfully disposed of your spouse's property, won't that be one more person who will be looking for you?

4. **If I don't have many items of personal property does that make relocation easier?**

Of course it makes things easier. Lighten your load by giving your soon-to-be-"ex" the stereo and the can opener. Get different stuff later.

Further, serial numbers on items of personal property (stereo, TV, VCR) are often a means of tracing missing persons.

5. **If I don't file for divorce but just disappear, is my spouse able to divorce me, or will we be married forever?**

Don't worry, your spouse could obtain a divorce in any state by filing in your absence. Typically, you would be served by having the Summons published a few times in the local newspaper and thirty days after the date of the final publication, you would be deemed to have been served. The court then has the jurisdiction to issue a judgment terminating the marriage and your spouse can proceed to obtain that decree by default procedures — that is, you did not reply to the published Summons so a divorce is given to your spouse in your absence.

The default process is a bit extra in price due to the cost of publication and usually takes a month or so longer in time. Start the divorce before you relocate as a favor to your spouse or, better yet, obtain the Final Judgment making you single before you relocate. The lighter you travel, the easier the trip.

6. **Can I start a new life with a new identity and still have contact with my kid(s)?**

Go back to Chapter One and reconsider the commitment necessary for a new identity and remind yourself that you cannot live two lives at once, rather you can only reshape the one you are living. You should understand that you are only able to choose sequential identities rather than multiple identities and that the sequential identities should not overlap.

Relocation at the expense of abandoning your kid(s) is unthinkable. I can certainly understand your decision never to see your friends or even old Uncle Fred again. But to walk out on a child is not the intended result of anything in this book.

Taking the child with you and hiding him or her from his or her other parent is equally wrong and it is a crime, if not a felony, in all states. See the story of Margot following this chapter for an illustration of how difficult and harmful a decision like that would be.

Children are the greatest reason why relocation under a new identity is not feasible for you. If a child is in your life, realize that your responsibility to that child is one of the highest callings you will ever have. Recommit to being the best parent for that child and give up any plans of abandonment by relocation. To leave your child would be a cruel form of child abuse.

7. **You mentioned "obligations" in the sense of financial obligations. Would cleaning up my debts prior to leaving be a good idea?**

It might. The ways of getting rid of debts are paying off those obligations, or by having those obligations discharged in bankruptcy. Just leaving them will not make the debts disappear, so if you ever resume your "old identity," those debts may still be enforceable and could have gained considerable interest and carrying charges. If it fits into your plans, bankruptcy may be strategically useful in that, like divorce, you leave with a clean slate.

Speaking of strategy, not only do you leave with a clean slate, but you have fewer people looking for you. Creditors, especially if they are owed money because of personal loans, will sometimes undertake searches to satisfy judgments or commence lawsuits for money owed.

8. How difficult is bankruptcy?

If you want to discharge consumer debts with a Chapter 7 petition, it is not difficult. On the other hand, if you have an ongoing business with large assets, large debts, and partners, you are looking at a much more complicated process.

9. How is bankruptcy accomplished?

You fill out a lengthy petition, make copies, enclose a filing fee, and submit the materials to a clerk of a bankruptcy court. Later, you will make one public appearance to answer any questions your creditors may have. Soon after, the debts are discharged and, between the filing and the final discharge, your creditors are forbidden from attempting any collection procedures.

The types of debts which are dischargeable include doctor bills, lawyer bills, credit card bills, personal loans, and payments on cars. Of course, the payments on cars are part of a secured transaction, so you would have to surrender the vehicle if you planned on not making the promised payments.

Paralegal services charge minimal fees to prepare the schedules and petition, as well as assist you with filing.

10. What are the drawbacks of bankruptcy?

First, there is a cost associated with preparation and filing.

Second, there is an effect on your credit but, in my experience, any loss of credit is short-lived. Further, if you will soon relocate under a new identity you would not be concerned with your "old" credit rating.

Third, be aware that not all debts are dischargeable. That is, the federal law that governs bankruptcy has made certain debts exempt from being able to be wiped out. Federal taxes are impossible to discharge, as are debts due to fraud, and obligations owed because of crimes. Other debts which will remain after bankruptcy are child support payments, debts due to willful injuries, fines, federally insured or guaranteed student loans, and drunk driving penalties. Therefore, if your principal debts and obligations are non-dischargeable, bankruptcy may be more cost and trouble that it will be worth.

Case History:
Margot, The Battered Wife

While many Americans think of leaving their jobs to live in New Zealand, Margot fled that idyllic, South Pacific country for California. With her, she brought her four-year-old son. She had come not for the weather and reputation of California, but for the anonymity she could have in a state with over twenty-five million people.

Nine years after she arrived in California, Margot came into my office and told her story: She had been in an extremely difficult marriage for about five years and had suffered both psychological and physical abuse. She described her New Zealand husband as a rich boy who grew up spoiled — never getting over periods of violent tantrums when he did not get his way. As a result, she had suffered beatings which had left her with broken bones.

"I did everything I was supposed to," Margot said in her accented voice. "I was the best wife and mother I could have been. His moods and violence were unpredictable." Margot told me that she also did everything by the book after the violence started: She reported him to the police, went to a shelter and obtained a restraining order, arranged for counseling and mediation meetings, then divorced him.

"When I saw that his violence would always be a part of my life, I knew I had to leave." Margot said that although there was a joint custody order she took the child. "Why play fair with a man that regularly beat me?" she said. "I took our boy and swore that I'd put some miles between us."

Margot went to Fiji with the boy for a "vacation," then boarded a flight to Hawaii, then flew on a domestic flight to California. The small nation of Fiji did not keep records of visiting New Zealanders that could be easily searched, so her trail went cold there. Further, her American entry point was Hawaii, so her trail was covered once again.

Within a year in California, she married an American and changed her name. All documentation except her New Zealand passport was reissued under her American married name. Nine years went by and she lived peacefully, only recently thinking of going back home to visit.

I told her that she had broken the law, specifically court orders allowing joint custody. Further, keeping the child out of contact with his father for nine years was not only cruel to the father but also cruel to the child. She answered with a shrug. My input during the next months was communication with a New Zealand barrister who smoothed the way for a recalling of the long-standing arrest warrant and negotiations for Margot's return to New Zealand after a ten-year absence.

CHAPTER THREE:
PERSONAL REORGANIZATION

1. Legal Name Changes

2. Common Law Name Changes

3. Credit Under a False Name

4. Marriage Under a False Name

5. False Personation

6. Fantasy Identity

7. False Professional or Honorary Status

8. Use of Another's Name

9. Improper Use of Another's Name

10. Name Change for a Minor

11. Unique Names

12. Prejudice Against an Alias

13. Excluding Evidence of an Alias

14. A Valid Excuse for an Alias

15. Definition of "Alias"

1.   **How can I go about changing my name?**

If you ask that question of a lawyer, he or she will tell you that you can file a petition with a court of competent jurisdiction. At the same time, you will be quoted a price for those services.

The process involves filling out and filing a petition, and often publishing the intent to petition for a name change. In California, the petitioner must publish at least three times and indicate the old name, as well as the new name. Of course, that requirement does something to the confidentiality of a new name choice. A court date is set to follow the publication, and the petitioner must appear in front of a judge to have the order signed. The order is then filed and becomes part of the court's records.

Be aware that missing person searchers look at court records in the jurisdiction where the missing person last lived. The point is that all the cost and effort spent on acquiring a new name will not guarantee any confidentiality.

2.   **Is that the only way to change my name?**

Not at all. Divorced women can petition to have their unmarried names restored.

There is also a method available to both men and women which is known as a "common law" name change and which consists of merely becoming known under a new name. That could be accomplished by simply having persons call you by that new name. That process is not illegal as long as the motives are not illegal.

Legal motives would include a woman's right to change her name due to marriage, or the modification of a name to make its spelling easier. Illegal motives would include obtaining credit under a false name and, therefore, under false pretenses.

3. Would it be illegal to receive bills under a new name?

As long as the bills were paid, I doubt if any creditor would care. Further, as long as the account was opened without the intent to defraud, there is an argument that there is no violation of the law. If the intent were proven, there could be the crime of obtaining credit under a false name.

4. Could I marry under a new name?

Yes, and the marriage would be valid. It would be illegal, however, to pose as another individual. That is, if you chose to be known by the name of a movie star, no law would be broken if that name identified you. It would be a felony, however, to pose as the movie star. That act, and other acts, are referred to in California as "false personation."

5. When would false personation be prosecuted?

In California, there are specific statutes in the Penal Code which punish posing as another to receive money, or posing as another to obtain a false credit report so as to obtain money or property. The aim of using a new name in those instances is not just assuming a new identity, but using that new identity to obtain money from others or to cheat them.

Many states also forbid falsely claiming to have a status for an advantage. For example, you may not falsely represent yourself as a veteran to solicit aid or to help you sell an item. Again, that is falsely claiming a status for an advantage or gain. You may not falsely represent yourself as a Catholic priest to seek donations, nor may you falsely say you are affiliated with a charity so as to solicit money or property.

Prosecution would likely take place when a new name is used to fool someone to obtain some advantage or money. It is unlikely that someone would be prosecuted for merely changing his name from Gomer to Joseph — who wouldn't? There the change was only a personal accommodation or preference and it should not matter that the change accompanied a relocation.

6. **Why can't I assume a new, fantasy identity?**

You may, as long as nobody is defrauded. The point is that changing from Gomer to Joseph is fine — you made a common law name change and you are entitled to do that. No law makes you stay "Gomer" all your life.

But you may not do so to fool someone into relying on you, or to gain a profit.

Also, with your "fantasy identity," are you going to pretend that you are something you are not? All states forbid the personation of peace officers, for example, as well as the exhibition of badges or emblems with the intent of inducing the belief that the holder is a peace officer. Many states forbid the unauthorized wearing of the badges of fraternal organizations, or the robes and apparel of religious denominations. You may call yourself Joseph, but not "Officer Joseph" or "Father Joseph." Using those names and titles is assuming a false status. Should authorities find that a fake Father Joseph is collecting for fictional missions in the Philippines, that is when they are most likely to prosecute.

I understand that a new name is a way to set something free in you and that the opportunity for a new identity possesses a riveting fascination. But you should not use a new identity to convince a woman in a bar that you are doing "secret government business," or that you are on a suicide mission for the CIA. Those juvenile fantasies are best left behind as they will call attention to you and create skepticism. Secondly, keep in mind that you must avoid profiting from any new name or assuming any false status by use of a new name.

7. **If I've had medical studies, can't I say I'm a doctor or a veterinarian? I've taken some law courses, so why can't I say I'm a lawyer?**

There you go again. Those representations would be the clearest examples of falsely claiming a status and would definitely be prosecuted.

Most states, in the exercise of their police power, provide for boards to certify persons seeking to be admitted to certain professions. The Medical Board of California, for example, has a division which is concerned with medical quality, a licensing division, and a division concerned with allied health professions. Each division has disciplinary powers and seeks to control the quality of the profession and thereby protect the public. In California, merely to use the initials "M.D." on your card so as to falsely imply you are a physician may make you guilty of a misdemeanor.

Professions are highly regulated. You may not "upgrade" your status in any way, nor can you assume a professional status when you are not licensed and allowed to do so. Not only would the licensing division prosecute you, but any "client" or "patient" would have reason to sue or prosecute. Again, realize that tall tales draw attention to yourself.

I can tell you the story of a man whose new identity was disclosed during the late seventies. He was a likable, law-abiding citizen whose mistake was that he falsely claimed to be the recipient of the Congressional Medal of Honor. Please understand that award is our highest military honor and is revered as practically sacred by military members, as well as civilians. When a friend became skeptical, a single call to a government registry revealed him as an impostor. Had he not embellished himself as a "hero," he would have remained secure in his new identity.

8. **What if I wanted to use the name of a movie star because I liked its sound and there would be no false assumption of the movie star's identity?**

    That would be okay because there is no property right in a personal name. You may be stopped from using the corporate and brand name of "General Motors," but you cannot be stopped from calling yourself "Bing Crosby," unless the personal name is used for improper purposes.

9. **What would be "improper" use of a personal name?**

    You already know about false personation, or false assumption of another's identity.

    A personal name may be improperly used to defraud or to invade another's privacy. For example, using the name Bing Crosby to falsely sell property "formerly owned by" the movie star, or to obtain information about the estate of Bing Crosby.

10. **Does a minor have a common law right to change his or her name?**

    No, although a parent or guardian may apply to the court on the minor's behalf for a legal name change. The petition must be signed by one of the parents, if living, or by the guardian, and both parents must receive notice of the petitioned change.

11. Could I change my name to something unique, such as a mathematical equation or a chemical symbol?

If you are considering doing something like that, I doubt if you are serious about successful relocation under a new identity.

Nevertheless, the California courts faced a similar situation in which an individual petitioned to legally change his name to the Roman numeral "III" (pronounced "Three"). *In re Richie* (1984) 159 CA 3d 1070, held that although there was no evidence indicating intent to defraud, the requested change did not constitute a "name" within the purview of the law. The court also considered that the usage of numbers or symbols for designating persons might cause confusion in public records.

Since the time of the Norman conquest, the common law has been that a legal name consists of one given name (first name) and one surname. Other designations, such as initials or titles ("Mrs.", "Jr.", "Dr.", or "Esq."), form no part of the legal name. Did you know that the film and recording star, Cher, found difficulty in legally changing her name to that single word because she was abandoning the use of a surname?

12. Doesn't the use of an alias give a bad impression?

Aliases evoke irrational disdain and it is especially bad for a criminal defendant to have evidence of alias use described to a jury, as it provides a prosecutor with the opportunity to emphasize consciousness of guilt. In *U.S. v. Wilkerson* (1972) 456 f2d 57, it was said, "People with nothing to hide do not use aliases." Moreover, aliases tend to indicate to the average mind that the user of the alias is a member of the criminal class and is therefore inherently suspect. Curiously, no such association is made when actors assume a "stage name."

The attorney who represents a client using an alias would be in flagrant violation of the oath of confidentiality by disclosing it. Further, once the prosecutor knows of an alias, the defense counsel should make a motion immediately to keep the jury from hearing that an alias was used.

13. On what grounds would evidence of an alias be kept from the jury?

The California case of *People v. Maroney* (1895) 109 C 277, shows understanding and an acknowledgment of the prejudicial effect of quoting an alias at trial. It is a case that recognizes the common law's lingering contempt for aliases and how that contempt can be an oppressive force to a defendant.

Secondly, *People v. DeHerrera* (1984) 680 p2d 848, challenges the relevancy of admitting evidence of an alias. In *DeHerrera*, the defendant was arrested just after an armed robbery which he may or may not have committed. Found on the defendant's person were two drivers licenses and a pay stub, all with different names. The Colorado Supreme Court said that evidence of alias use should not be allowed unless it is relevant to the issue. That is, whether or not Mr. DeHerrera used an alias has nothing to do with whether or not he committed the robbery.

14. What do you tell people who challenge you to provide a valid excuse for an alias?

During the 1950s, Rudolph Schware, a Jew, had been denied permission by the New Mexico Board of Bar Examiners to take the bar examination, in large part because he had used aliases from 1934 to 1937 and that was seen as a reflection on his moral fitness to practice law. Schware showed that he used those aliases to obtain jobs in industries which discriminated against Jews. He also did labor organization, recruiting non-Jewish employees where he worked.

In the U.S. Supreme Court, in the case of *Schware v. Board of Bar Examiners* (1957) 353 U.S. 232, it was said that, "Of course it is wrong to use an alias when it is done to cheat or defraud another, but it can hardly be said that attempts to forestall anti-Semitism or to organize workers was [sic] wrong."

15. What does "alias" mean?

It is the Latin word for "otherwise." The longer phrase, "alias dictus," was used to indicate that a person was otherwise called by one or the other of two names.

Case History:
Frank, Alias Mr. Hyde

I first met Frank in a county jail visiting room where he was wearing an orange, jail-issued jumpsuit and was waiting to be arraigned on petty theft charges. He had asked me to represent him as he did not qualify for public defender representation — he made about $75,000 per year and had too much money. He was an immediate mystery to me because he had been arrested trying to leave Denny's without paying for a $4.25 breakfast.

Next, Frank confided in me that he had prior arrests for petty theft under other names and he did not want the police to know about them. I informed him that any information he gave me was confidential and that I felt the use of an alias, to be evidence of consciousness of guilt, should follow rather than precede the present crime. I then asked him why a middle-class person would steal breakfast and why he used aliases.

"Did you ever read *The Strange Case of Dr. Jekyll and Mr. Hyde*?" he asked. I said I had not but that I was familiar with the story. "It's not just a monster story," he said, "it's about the duality of human nature — opposing forces trapped within the same person."

Frank told me that he always felt that part of him was "unexpressed." After all, he never had a vote about being born or choosing his name. Therefore, his use of aliases and commission of petty crimes like shoplifting were an articulation of something else inside of him. "Just get me a fine as if this were a first offense," he said as he gave me a pat on the shoulder.

Later that week, I found a copy of the story he had mentioned and found a passage about Dr. Jekyll's reaction when for the first time he sees the other side of his nature in the mirror:

"And yet when I looked upon that ugly idol in the glass, I was conscious of no repugnance, rather of a leap of welcome. This too, was myself. It seemed natural and human ..."

CHAPTER FOUR:
NEW IDENTITY PAPERS

1. Making False Documents

2. Falsifying Certificates

3. Out-of-State Drivers Licenses

4. Licenses issued under AKAs

5. Tracing from AKA Identity to Original Identity

6. Using Another's Birth Certificate

7. Obtaining Documents

8. Obtaining Another's Birth Certificate

9. Duplicate Social Security Card

10. New Social Security Numbers

11. Obtaining Another's Identity

12. New Social Security Account

13. New Social Security for an Infant

14. Displaying False Identification to an Officer

15. False Name to an Officer

16. Additional Identity Papers

1. **Could I create documents which identify me by my new name?**

Not only is the use of false documents forbidden, but the manufacture, whether for personal use or for sale, of government identification papers is forbidden. Therefore, the printing of a fake drivers license, or altering your existing one, is a misdemeanor.

The practical considerations of creating false documentation involve needing the proper technical skills and having the appropriate equipment. Are you a printer and do you have access to printing equipment? Further, many states have adopted special, tamper-proof paper for drivers licenses so a convincing counterfeit is practically impossible.

2. **How about falsifying a birth certificate or a baptismal certificate?**

Those are documents which would be easier to counterfeit, but California law, and the law of most states, specifically forbids the manufacture of either of those documents if the manufacturer knows that the intent is to deceive. California also makes it a misdemeanor to have a counterfeit certificate of birth or a counterfeit certificate of baptism in your possession.

3. **Can I go to another state and obtain a drivers license?**

That would be a better idea than making or obtaining a fake drivers license. Typically, you would present your old, out-of-state license as identification. If you claimed not to have an out-of-state license, you would be asked to identify yourself with a birth certificate and a social security number. Those items of identification, together with an application fee and success on any driving test, would get you a new drivers license from another state.

Of course, the second state would continue to use your old name.

4. **Can I legally request that a new name be put on my new, out-of-state drivers license?**

   In many states, yes. California allows its drivers to have licenses issued under AKAs. The procedure involves applying for a license under a new name and an AKA affidavit is filled out and kept on file. There is no additional charge.

   The AKA affidavit is kept on file at the local Department of Motor Vehicles; it is not forwarded to the Secretary of State. Therefore, this procedure gives you a new license with a new name and no laws have been broken. If you are not the subject of an active search and as long as you are not using an AKA for deception, this above-board procedure is worthy of consideration. You could relocate to a state allowing AKAs and be known under that assumed name without breaking any laws.

5. **Couldn't my old (original) name be discovered?**

   Yes, if an individual did the right sort of search. Consider this: If someone wrote a local check which was printed with the name, "John Smith," and then presented the check for cashing with a valid drivers license for that state identifying the check writer as John Smith, and if the signatures matched, the person being asked to cash the check would not be likely to call the Department of Motor Vehicles to search for an AKA affidavit.

   In other words, a valid license issued under an AKA would be fine for day-to-day exchanges and business.

6. **Could I obtain someone else's birth certificate and Social Security number, then apply for an out-of-state drivers license under that identity?**

You already know that it would be illegal. If you attempted to do so in spite of my advice, you would need to consider the following: (1) You would want the "donor" identity to be similar in age, gender, and racial characteristics; (2) You would want the "donor" to be cooperative and, for that reason, it has been said that the best donor is someone recently deceased; and (3) You would need both those items of identification.

7. **Could I "borrow" those documents from a friend or a relative?**

That would be a convenient "package deal" but you have more considerations to follow: (1) It would not be wise to borrow those documents from a living person still in the workforce as there would be two incomes reported on his or her Social Security account, given that you were both in the workforce; (2) Any trouble for either of you (criminal/domestic/IRS) could cause trouble for the other, perhaps even being taken into custody; and (3) The use of a dead relative/friend's identity and then trouble in your life (criminal/medical emergency) could lead to a report to the "donor's" parents or next-of-kin and reveal your relocation and new identity.

8. **Then I may want to obtain the birth certificate of a stranger. How can that be done?**

An official certificate of every birth, death, marriage, and divorce should be on file in the locality where the event occurred. The Federal Government does not maintain files or indexes of these records although they do maintain federal criminal files. Records of births are filed permanently either in a State vital statistics office, or in a city, county, or other local office.

Let your fingers do the walking and look up the government offices in the phone book for the county in which the individual was born. You may try under "County Recorder" or "Hall of Records."

To obtain a certified copy of a birth certificate, you can apply in person or by mail. If by mail, write to the appropriate office and include the appropriate fee by money order or certified check. Be aware that fees are subject to change. Ask for a copy of the birth certificate and supply the following information: (1) The full name of the person whose record is being requested; (2) The sex and race; (3) The parents' names, including the maiden name of the mother; (4) The date of birth; (5) The purpose for which the copy is needed; and (6) Your relationship to the person whose record is being requested.

You would be supplying false information and possibly breaking the law to inform the agency holding the birth certificate that you were the subject of the certificate. That is, it would be fraudulent to say, "I am Bob Jones and I need a copy of my birth certificate so I may obtain a passport."

9. **How may I obtain a duplicate Social Security card?**

People lose their wallets and identity papers every day and this problem is common. A call to your local Social Security office will inform you that you can go into the office, fill out an application for a duplicate card, identify yourself with a credit card, and a duplicate card will be mailed to you in a few weeks. There is no charge.

That process, of course, is to receive a duplicate card for an existing account. It may be more difficult to apply for a new account. Should you apply for a new account number, identification will be asked for.

10. I have a birth certificate for identification. Can I go to a Social Security office and apply for a new Social Security number?

The birth certificate is good identification and would, in addition, verify your date of birth. Social Security may ask for a drivers license, if you have one. I have been told that they will settle for almost anything with your name on it, including a credit card.

11. I am thinking of locating a same-age, same-gender, same-race individual who just passed away and obtaining both that person's birth certificate and Social Security number. Any problems?

All of that is possible, but you would be breaking the law.

Your scheme reminds me of an acquaintance who "relocated" to escape from a gang contract on his life. He obtained his new name from a recent obituary in a San Francisco newspaper — a publication that, unfortunately, lists young and middle-age men dying every day. The obituary gave the place of birth and the names of the late man's family members. A single phone call to a relative listed in the obituary, together with some explanations how the caller was a "long-lost relative," gave him the mother's maiden name. He applied for a birth certificate and, on the same day, applied for a credit card through the mail under the deceased's name. The credit card and the birth certificate both arrived on the same day and the man seeking to relocate used both those documents to obtain a duplicate social security card for the existing account of the deceased man. One month later, he relocated from California to Texas and obtained a drivers license using the birth certificate and Social Security card of the deceased man. I can only assume that Social Security authorities believe that the San Francisco man never died, instead that he relocated to Texas where he is working and paying into the Social Security account for that number.

12. Is it possible to apply for a Social Security number which is a new account?

That would be easy to do if you are an infant or a young child. Of course, if you are age twenty-five to sixty, there would be questions about why you do not have an existing account.

Some people have just replied that they never did have a number assigned to them and have been successful with that story. Other individuals have offered more elaborate stories why they have not been in the workforce and, therefore, do not have an existing account.

I was told of one individual who went to a Social Security office wearing a Roman collar and bearing both a birth certificate for a same-age, same-gender, same-race person, as well as a forged letter from a Catholic diocese stating that he was soon leaving the religious order. His explanation for not having a Social Security number was that he had entered the seminary at age eighteen and had been a member of the religious order ever since.

I have also been told of another individual who went to Social Security with a companion, then presented a birth certificate and another sort of letter — a letter from a psychologist explaining that the applicant was intellectually and/or emotionally impaired and had not worked during his life. Placing the individual into society (main-streaming) was the current therapy for the applicant and, accordingly, the applicant needed a Social Security card to obtain employment in a fast-food restaurant. The companion informed the Social Security clerk that he was the applicant's brother and proceeded to assist with filling out the forms.

While both of the above do provide logical reasons why an adult would not have an existing Social Security account, be aware that both of those claims would be fraudulent and illegal if they were untrue.

13. What if I applied for a Social Security number for my child and then used that number? What if I "invented" a child and applied for a Social Security number?

Either way you would be committing a fraud and either way you would need a birth certificate for the "child." It would, however, provide you with a new account.

14. What if I showed a drivers license with a false identity to the police?

If you were to use falsified documents to avoid police authorities, your conduct and statements, if indicating a consciousness of guilt, would be relevant and admissible against you. The use of false statements as to identity — including a physical disguise and/or the assumption of a false name — could arguably be seen as resisting arrest, or flight after the commission of a crime.

People v. Bertholf (1963) 221 CA 2d 599, held that intentional fabrications designed to prevent connection with a criminal act are admissible as evidence of consciousness of guilt. *People v. Sieveri* (1967) 255 CA 2d 34, held that any false statement, if not otherwise inadmissible, may be used to show consciousness of guilt.

15. What if I give a false name to the police and I am not wanted, nor guilty of any crime?

California Penal Code s. 148.9 provides that falsely representing or identifying yourself as another person, or as a fictitious person, to a law enforcement officer upon a lawful arrest, or even during a time of detention, either to evade the process of the court, or to evade proper identification, is a misdemeanor.

If you presented the peace officer with a legal license issued under an AKA affidavit, it would be arguable that you are not providing falsified documents as the license was issued by the DMV, nor are you presenting yourself as a fictitious person. That is, the AKA name does, in fact, indicate you. Should the officer ask, "Is this your true name?," or, "Have you ever been known by any other names?" you would be obligated at that time to inform the officer that the license indicates an AKA.

16. Would there be any use for additional identity papers?

Some people consider collateral identification papers useful in firming-up a new identity. For example, many "diploma-by-mail" enterprises advertise in the backs of magazines. For a price and little effort, you can acquire a diploma issued under your new name. Likewise, certain trade certificates can be gained through the mail.

Remember, inconsistent identification papers are one problem in establishing a new identity. That is, carrying a drivers license issued to "John Smith," along with a diploma issued to "Jack Brown," as well as credit cards under two other names, would lead to suspicion. Additional identity papers are fine but they should be consistent with your new name.

Case History:
Bobby, In Fear for His Life

Bobby skippered a charter yacht on Oahu, Hawaii, and during the evenings he waited tables at a restaurant and sold cocaine to his friends. Everything was terrific in Paradise until one day he got a frantic call that his cocaine supplier had just been found dead in his car. Bobby knew immediately that he was next.

"It was time for a witness relocation program right then and there," Bobby said to me after years of hiding in California. "I didn't even go back to my apartment. I drove to the airport and put my locked pickup in an outer parking lot. At the airport, five minutes before my flight, I called a safe friend and said I was going upcountry (the highlands) on Maui for awhile and he could come and get my truck. I told him where it was and that I'd mail him the key from one of the airport souvenir shops. Five minutes later, I was on my way to California with one change of clothes and $300 in my wallet."

He reminisced over coffee about his first tough year in California, working at a gas station. "It was a low-level job, but easy to get without references and I was hired on a first-name basis. A gas station is also a good place to pick up cheap, clunker cars that you can drive for a while without registration or insurance."

When I asked if he really thought he had been in danger, he made a serious face and nodded. Bobby said that he had been a part of a theft of cocaine from his supplier's supplier. "I knew we'd been found out and I knew how they'd deal with me. Do I care about the clothes and stuff in my apartment? It was worth giving up so I didn't get a bullet in my head."

Bobby used a California AKA license for one year, then obtained a birth certificate of a recently deceased man, coincidentally named Robert. Soon, Bobby was using the dead man's identity, including his Social Security number. A couple more years have clicked by and Bobby has relaxed, although he has kept his new identity. His feeling of security is helped by the belief that the people after him are probably in prison or dead.

"My secret," said Bobby, "was a complete lifestyle change: No sailing; no waterfront nightlife; no cocaine. I'm sure the change saved my life."

CHAPTER FIVE:
TRACING MISSING PERSONS

1. The Search Industry

2. General Methods of Search

3. Searching Court Records

4. Search Protection

5. Searching Auto Registration

6. Keeping Your Vehicle

7. Search of Credit Bills

8. Posters and Photos

9. Cost of Searches

10. Search of Phone Bills

11. Reverse Directory Search

12. Social Security Number Search

1. **Are searches made for missing persons, or does that only happen in the movies?**

There are agencies and private businesses who search for missing persons, as well as investigators who locate assets, make financial reports on third parties, do background reports about employees, carry out surveillance, and attempt to recover children wrongfully taken from custodial parents. Probate attorneys must make diligent searches in trying to locate all heirs. Litigation attorneys try to locate witnesses, policy holders, and beneficiaries who have moved and left no forwarding address. The search industry is large and sophisticated.

2. **What methods do investigators use to search for missing persons?**

The methods vary from the simple to the sophisticated. One of the most direct and economical is to talk with the friends, relatives, and workmates of the missing person and to ask if the missing party discussed plans to leave, or fantasized about another location. At the same time, there would be questions about known enemies, gambling debts, and things like that. The cardinal rule of relocation under a new identity — as discussed in Chapter One — is to shut up about any such plans.

A second method of search is to check public records, which may include directory assistance, voter's registration, real property registrations at the Recorder's Office, and court records.

A third method of search would be to check the personal records of the missing party, such as utility bills. Occasionally, investigators run credit checks.

3. **What would a search of court records reveal?**

Well, for one thing it would reveal a legal name change done by petition to the court. From that information, the investigator would search under the missing person's birth name, as well as the AKA.

All but the smallest counties now have court filings, both criminal and civil, indexed on microfilm. Any citizen can go to the courthouse and request filings for a certain period, then search for any particular litigant. The index is organized, of course, in alphabetical order, so, once again, the name of the missing party is important.

4. **How can I be protected from those three methods of searching?**

You already know that it's best to keep your plans to yourself. It only takes one person to identify you or locate you. A new identity in an unknown location is the next best way to thwart searches of records. Likewise, a search of accounts won't hit if the name of the account holder is unknown.

5. **Why didn't you mention searches of automobile registrations?**

In 1989, actress Rebecca Schaeffer was shot to death on her doorstep by a stalker who tracked her through state automobile records. Prior to that incident, the phenomenon of stalking gained wide notice in 1982, when actress Theresa Saldana survived a brutal knife attack from a crazed fan. Likewise, in 1988 Richard Wade Farley gunned down eleven people in Sunnyvale, California, because one of them had rebuffed his advances. Since those incidents, more than two dozen states have adopted anti-stalking laws, and California has passed a law restricting access to individual Department of Motor Vehicle files.

Those records, however, may be obtained by licensed investigators or by court order.

6. Then is it okay to keep my car and take it to the location of my new identity?

That would be a big mistake. Just because vehicle registration searches are more difficult at this time does not mean they are impossible.

Secondly, consider that out-of-state license plates always draw attention — the smaller the town the more attention. People will be asking you about where you are from and what it was like in your previous state.

Third, you may like your vehicle because it is an "old friend," feels familiar, and is reliable, but your vehicle can identify you. Each of us drives a distinctive vehicle — a brown pickup with a dent; a silver Honda with blacked-out windows; a red Corvette with loud exhaust — and the distinctiveness can be trouble.

The point is, your old car always gets left behind with your old identity. America has plenty of cars and you'll always find another — maybe one better suited to the new geography. If you are traveling internationally you won't be keeping your old car.

7. Are there still other methods of search?

There are as many methods as the investigator's imagination will create. Another method is to review credit card bills if those accounts are still open and being used.

During the mid-1980s, I was contacted by a father who had serious concerns about his son. The son had left work at lunchtime and never returned for the afternoon shift.

The son's expensive car was found abandoned in a Safeway parking lot and there was the possibility of foul play.

The father believed he needed to be appointed as his son's conservator, as the younger, unmarried man had been missing for two weeks and bills needed to be paid, as well as accounts managed while the son was being searched for. An investigator was hired and I assisted in establishing a conservatorship.

The mystery was partially solved after another week, when credit card statements came in the mail and showed a trail of lodgings and meals at motels down California and across Arizona and New Mexico. We then knew that someone was using the son's credit cards — either the son or a thief.

The investigator anticipated the next destinations and alerted the police with photos. An alert patrolman located the son and the young man willingly agreed to return to his hometown, explaining that he had left partly as a "lark" and partly because he felt he was having a "breakdown."

8. **So, are "wanted posters" and photos another method of searching for missing persons?**

Information and photos have been put on milk cartons for quite some time to assist with the locating and return of missing children. Some investigators also employ the distribution of recent photos to try to locate missing adults.

A requirement for that method is to have a specific location in mind, unless the display of the photos is to a nationwide audience. The investigator would want to know the location of the last appearance of the missing person, or the anticipated destination of the missing person.

Therefore, your own appearance is a consideration if you decide to create a new identity, and changing your appearance will be discussed in the following chapter.

9.   How much do professional searches cost?

Less than you might think. A "due diligence" search is a minimum effort search to fulfill the requirements of substituted service and is only about $250. A more complicated search effort using a few more of the search methods we have discussed could be as inexpensive as $350. The point is that tracing missing persons is possible by a private party with only modest resources.

10. What other private records could be used to track me?

The most obvious would be to intercept the monthly phone bill of a close friend or loved one. Sure, the theft of a letter is illegal, but is easily effected by taking it from Aunt Maude's curbside mailbox, or even from her front porch, then returning it after it was opened and inspected. As you see, that is a good example why a letter slot in the front door so the letter drops inside is a better method of mail delivery.

The person inspecting the phone bill would review the monthly long-distance calls made from Aunt Maude's phone. One of the phone numbers might lead to the person being sought.

11. Can a location be found with just a phone number?

Yes, by reference to a "reverse directory."

Law enforcement agencies, as well as utility companies, have use of directories that give names and addresses according to number. That is the opposite, of course, of the directory that is supplied to the average household with a telephone. These directories often include phone numbers that are unlisted in the normal phone books.

12. How can a person be contacted through a Social Security number?

The Social Security agency may locate you if an employer is paying deducted funds into your account.

The agency also offers a letter-forwarding service that not many people know about and which allows family members to locate a "lost" relative who is still in the workforce. As stated above, an employer must turn in the Social Security number of employees, as well as deduction records. The family of the missing individual may write a letter and put it in an unsealed envelope, then submit it to an Social Security office together with a written request for the forwarding service. To qualify for the assistance, the family must claim to have been out of touch for at least nine months. The Social Security Administration is not required to report to the family if the letter has been claimed, so, in that way, the contact is one-way.

Case History:
Barnwell, The Private Eye

Most investigators are bright and have military and/or police experience. Barnwell had all of that and, in addition, was attending law school at night when I first met him. He described his investigative work as one-third surveillance for industry, one-third surveillance on domestic matters, and the remaining third was a mixture of jobs which included only the occasional missing person search.

"I did one search for a girlfriend who got deserted and was furious. The ex-boyfriend was easy to find because he made two mistakes: He didn't go very far and he didn't change his habits. The client said he was a good pool player, always playing pool. So I just went to a few of the neighboring towns and showed his picture around the pool halls. They may have told him someone was looking for him, but he didn't seem to care because he kept showing up to shoot pool. I followed him home and gave his address to my client. I heard she tore his place apart."

Barnwell did another search that involved a missing person who changed his identity. Barnwell's client was the last employer of the missing person and they informed Barnwell that the missing person wrongfully took several thousand dollars worth of the employer's tools when he left. "I decided that a search for his vehicle should not be overlooked as a possibility because he could not transport so many tools without a truck. More importantly, I decided that if he wanted the tools he would probably use them — in other words, he probably planned to continue his career using the ex-employer's tools. So I decided to search through the Department of Consumer Affairs because the missing person was licensed as a contractor through the Contractors' State License Board. Sure enough, he renewed his license and bond under his own name and I got an address in Northern California for him. We recovered every single tool that the client said was missing."

CHAPTER SIX:
CHANGING YOUR LOOKS

1.   The Right to Alter Your Looks

2.   The Right to Plastic Surgery

3.   New Wardrobe

4.   Tattoo Removal

5.   Identification That Cannot Be Disguised

1. **As part of a new identity, I've decided to change my looks. Is that against the law?**

    Of course not. Police authorities or private parties who are looking for you may try to describe it as furtive conduct and therefore indicative of guilt or responsibility, but nothing prohibits individuality in appearance and the right to change your appearance.

2. **Is plastic surgery (cosmetic surgery) an option?**

    Again, if you have adult status, you have the right to choose surgical procedures, but I think something like that would be drastic. Why not simply lose or gain weight, cut or grow your hair, and acquire a new wardrobe?

3. **Why do you suggest a new wardrobe to go with a new identity?**

    Your clothes may be as identifiable as the car you drive and investigators often inquire about the apparel of the missing person.

    If you wear distinctive clothing, be aware that it will impress others. For example, that cowboy hat was fine in Wyoming but is going to be conspicuous in New York. Likewise, those lime-green pants you wore back in Florida are out of place in Washington.

4. **Is tattoo removal "too drastic"?**

    Police officers often say that tattoos are one of the best methods of identification, especially if there are multiple tattoos. For that reason, and others, I think that acquiring a visible tattoo is a mistake. It's an irony that prisoners who are frequent offenders often indulge in "body art" and make themselves much more conspicuous and identifiable.

Therefore, tattoo removal is worthy of consideration and is usually not the same sort of invasive surgical procedure as a nose job. Further, if a tattoo is a reminder of old, bad habits (marijuana leaf or racist insignia) it's removal may be appropriate for a really new identity.

5. **Is there any part of my looks that cannot be disguised?**

Interestingly, the shape and contours of your ears are details that cannot easily be changed and investigators often compare photos of ears to identify a missing person.

The California case of *People v. Marx* (1975) 54 CA 3d 100, makes bite marks admissible to identify a defendant. Dental identification through forensic dentistry is based on the theory that because human adults have thirty-two teeth, each with five anatomic surfaces, there are 160 dental surfaces that may contain identifying characteristics and which create the individuality of your dentition. In addition, facial structure, occlusion, and the shape of the teeth and jaw also identify and are difficult to disguise.

Fingerprint examination (dactylography) is a science with which we are all familiar and which rests on the basis that fingerprints are unchanging, unique, and transferable to some surfaces. The friction ridges that leave fingerprint impressions are found on the fingers and the palmar surfaces and the almost universal belief is that the ridge pattern never changes during life. If you should abrade or lacerate the fingers up to one millimeter in depth, there will be a temporary scar but the original pattern will return after healing. Therefore fingerprints cannot be disguised.

Advances in serology during the past few decades have created a virtual revolution in the analysis of genetic markers, including blood determinations. Analysis of your blood will describe your sex, some genetic markers which will identify your race, and your blood group. Identification tests on your white blood cells (leukocytes) have an error rate of only 0.35%. Red cell enzymes and serum proteins may be identified. Sperm antibodies may be present in your system. Finally, DNA typing is a foolproof procedure for identification whereby the unique DNA "fingerprint" of an individual is mapped. The total of your genetic markers is unchanging and impossible to alter.

With modern technology, you could never erase all of the identification possibilities, so I do not think that drastic measures should be taken. Miss Clairol would be fine; plastic surgery would be too much.

Case History:
Abbie Hoffman, On the Lam

Abbie Hoffman, the political activist and member of the Chicago Eight, found himself discontent with his life a few years into the decade of the Seventies. He vacationed at St. Thomas, V.I., and used one of the sets of phony I.D.s he had stored away, opening a bank account and renting a house under an alias. He had a new baby (named "America") and fell in love with the relaxation he found in the area of the Caribbean.

Months later and back in New York, Hoffman was taken into custody on a cocaine charge and spent time in the Tombs, facing trial and a potential fifteen-year sentence. At that time, he remembered the peace he had found in the Caribbean and decided that if he ever got out on bail, he would just "keep going."

During February of 1974, Hoffman did get out on bail and had friends inquire into foreign countries' attitudes about allowing him to stay for a prolonged time. Hoffman himself went to Europe and Mexico while on bail, then decided on a destination he did not disclose in his 1980 book, *Soon To Be A Major Motion Picture*. He handed letters to a friend to be sent from various cities to create a false trail. His first stop was Atlanta where his curly, dark hair was processed straight, then died blonde. He sat down in his motel room and practiced his new identity by writing the story of his "new" life.

Hoffman flew to Los Angeles to have cosmetic surgery on his face, then flew to his new, secret home. He lived six years "on the lam," as he said, and published the above-referenced book in 1980 wherein he said that he lived in small towns, taught school, took classes at night, and kept a low profile. During that time, he was aware that the police continued to look for him, even conducting raids on communes, keeping watch on his friends, and infiltrating his father's funeral.

In the Spring of 1975, Hoffman gave an interview to *Playboy* magazine which foolishly revealed his whereabouts. He fled to Canada, then to Chicago, of all places.

The strain of hiding for years was immense and the once-fearless activist was burdened by the pressures of hiding, even thinking of suicide and suffering periods of mental strain — calling himself a "controlled schizophrenic." He sought peace in Northern California and, for a time, found clarity while writing, working for environmental concerns, and still challenging authority. Sadly, his death came some years later and it was believed to be a suicide.

CHAPTER SEVEN: POLICE SEARCHES

1. **I've had some trouble with the criminal justice system and I'd like to leave it behind me. Will the police search for me?**

It depends on what the "trouble" was. After all, there is a difference between having outstanding traffic warrants and being on the Ten-Most-Wanted list.

The likely way that the police would get their hands on you, if you were using your correct name and corresponding identification, would be to run your name through a warrant check after asking you to identify yourself. If warrants were present, the name would "hit" and you would be taken into custody. In that situation, there was no active search, yet the result was the same as a successful investigation.

2. **Which police personnel do warrant checks?**

The patrolmen in the field usually do not have the hardware to conduct a warrant search, so he or she will call in a name and the search will be done by the dispatcher.

3. **At what level are searches carried out by dispatchers?**

At the local, the state, and national levels. If the computer is up and running, all three levels of search can be completed in less than three minutes.

4. **Then the name I give the patrolman would have to be the same as the name in the warrant?**

As a general rule, the closer the search the more the spelling has to be correct. That is, local searches must have the exact spelling and not just the same-sounding name. State authorities, however, have different-spell searches and can hit on sound-alike names.

5. **Will all warrants automatically turn up?**

   A national search will pick up warrants anywhere in the
   U.S.A., if the source of the warrant (the issuing jurisdiction) puts the warrant into the computer. A low-level
   property crime (malicious mischief or vandalism) might
   not be included while a warrant for serious, anti-person
   behavior would almost certainly be.

6. **If a warrant turns up, will I be taken into custody and
   extradited back to the jurisdiction issuing the warrant?**

   The Constitution contains a provision that a "person
   charged in any state with treason, felony, or other crime,
   who shall flee from justice, and be found in another state,
   shall, on demand of the executive authority of the state
   from which he fled, be delivered up, to be removed to the
   state having jurisdiction of the crime."

   For more than a century the Supreme Court nullified that
   constitutional requirement with the decision of *Kentucky
   v. Dennison* (1861) 24 How. 66 which said that the gover-
   nor of Ohio did not have a legal compulsion to surrender
   a fugitive who had been indicted for helping a slave to escape to the north, although there may be a moral obliga-
   tion to do so.

   The ineffectiveness of that clause was offset by the enact-
   ment of a federal law making it a crime to flee from state
   to state to avoid prosecution and the adoption, by most
   states, of a uniform extradition act.

   In 1987, the *Kentucky* holding was discarded, being declared to be "the product of another time" and reflecting a
   relationship between the states which showed coopera-
   tion. In *Puerto Rico v. Branstad* (1987) 483 U.S. 219, it was
   held that the courts could indeed compel the surrender of
   an extradited fugitive. Therefore, the states of the U.S. are

not adverse, coequal sovereigns — each will yield to the extradition wishes of the others.

Once again, it depends on what your "trouble" was. Some jurisdictions will extradite to only certain locations. Other jurisdictions will make a case-by-case cost-benefit analysis on whether or not to extradite. Certain crimes, you can understand, are just not worthy of extradition efforts.

7. **Are there other methods of police searches?**

Of course. You've seen wanted posters at the post office and, in recent years, the electronic media have begun broadcasting docudramas about fugitives.

A more day-to-day method of search, however, is to check the serial numbers of private property, such as a stereo or a television. That sort of search can not only reveal evidence of a crime, but can also show the identity of the person in possession.

8. **Am I able to alter serial numbers on items of private property?**

The California Penal Code allows you to deface or alter the serial numbers if you are the owner of the property.

9. **How long do police agencies search for missing or wanted persons?**

That depends, of course, on the nature of the crime and/or the notoriety of the wanted/missing person.

In Chapter Ten, there is the description of an eighteen-year FBI search for the escaped felon, Bill Allen. The short answer to your question is that police authorities may search for you forever.

10. What items of information will the police most likely ask about a missing person?

They will ask for a physical description which will include:

1. Gender
2. Age
3. Height & Weight
4. Color of Eyes & Hair
5. Ethnicity
6. Distinguishing Marks

They will also ask for a "social description" of the missing person which will include:

1. Name
2. I.D. Papers (Drivers License & S.S.#)
3. Vehicle (year/make/model/license number)
4. Clothes last wearing
5. Where last employed
6. Where going at time of disappearance
7. Hobbies & Pastimes
8. Friends & Relatives

Case History:
Detective Michael

"Much police work is based on a single premise about human nature: People do the same things over and over." Mike is a friend and detective who gave me the above quote during a sandwich-and-beer lunch date. "You see," said Mike, "we are all creatures of routine. If a detective can divine a perp's routines, he's closer to being caught."

I explained to Mike that I wanted his views on searching for a criminal suspect who was missing, or a plain missing person. "Same thing," he said. "Take the Son of Sam case in New York, for example: Here was a guy who frustrated the police for months, striking at random, leaving few clues. The nature of the crimes (shooting young women or couples in parked cars) made it just impossible to predict when he would hit next. But the guy was caught when cops ran registration checks on cars that were ticketed in that area during the night of one shooting. Son of Sam drove his own car to the murder scene — the way he would drive to the office — and that routine behavior nailed him."

Mike said that most detectives would take a physical description as well as a "social description" of a wanted person (see #10, Chapter 7). The social routines were just as important as the height-and-weight statistics because they could place the person at certain locations at certain times.

Mike then said that so-called "friends" are often a missing person's undoing, providing lots of information about location and habits. "The perp is stupid but wants recognition, wants glamour. He's made sure that everyone has seen his gun — probably has waved it around at a party, like he's in a movie. When we talk to the girls who were at the party, they all tell us, 'He's got a gun.' When we ask 'Where's he headed?' some of them can tell us because the perp was stupid enough to tell them." So what's the second premise about human nature? "People don't know when to keep their mouths shut," says Mike.

CHAPTER EIGHT:
THE RIGHT TO TRAVEL

1. Right of Interstate Travel

2. Limitations on Interstate Travel

3. Effect of Parole on Travel

4. Right of International Travel

5. Right to Own a Passport

6. Obtaining a Passport

7. Government Benefits Abroad

8. Travel Without a Passport

9. Foreign Country Choices

10. Obtaining a Passport Under a New Identity

1. **Under what right am I free to relocate?**

The right to *interstate* travel is a part of the "liberty" that citizens of America cannot be deprived of without the due process of law. It is guaranteed by the Due Process Clause of the Constitution and is a fundamental aspect of your liberty. *Shapiro v. Thompson* (1969) 394 U.S. 618.

2. **Can the right to interstate travel ever be limited?**

Yes, by the "due process" of law mentioned above.

For example, a Georgia law made abandonment of a dependent child a misdemeanor, but raised the offense to a felony if the parent committed the offense and then left the state. The constitutionality of that law was challenged in the U.S. Supreme Court in *Jones v. Helms* (1981) 452 U.S. 412, and it was held that the Georgia law was valid and enacted under due process.

Therefore, a government cannot stop or penalize the right to freely travel interstate. Laws that blatantly did so would be impermissible. However, the Georgia statute can make an allowable prohibition on travel because it aggravates the consequences of conduct that is otherwise punishable. In other words, the U.S. Supreme Court has said that states may treat interstate flight to abandon children as serious, antisocial behavior which may be punished. That punishment is not unconstitutional because it infringes on the right to travel. Rather, due process was met and the punishment was valid.

3. **Can the status of parole take away my right to interstate travel?**

Certainly. Being on parole means living by a code of conduct prescribed by the parole authorities and every state releases parolees only after a written notice of parole is presented to the inmate.

The California Administrative Code advises of general conditions of parole and requires that parolees must comply with all instructions of the assigned parole agent, including a prohibition on travel over fifty miles from the parolee's residence without the agent's prior approval. Parolees in California are not to be absent from their county of residence for a period of more than forty-eight hours and cannot leave the State of California without prior written approval. Title 15, s. 2512(3).

4. **How about *international* travel? Am I free to travel to any other country?**

Yes, if you have a passport and your intended area of travel is not restricted.

The federal Passport Act (22 U.S.C. s. 211(a)) was derived from an early American law and provides that the Secretary of State may grant and issue passports under rules prescribed by the President. Although that federal law does not mention areas where you cannot go, certain restrictions have been common both in peacetime and wartime. The Act — the basis for modern passport administration — allows the State Department to deny travel documents to applicants with criminal records and to noncitizens.

From 1917 to 1931, passports were refused to members of the American Communist Party. The 1950 McCarran Act forbade members of any Communist organization to apply for or use a passport.

Before 1961, no passport was required for Western Hemisphere travel. That is, you could visit those countries merely carrying a birth certificate or an official letter of introduction. When the U.S.A. broke diplomatic relations with Cuba and the Department of State forbade travel to Cuba, an appeal was brought before the U.S. Supreme Court saying that the federal orders were invalid because they infringed on the fundamental right to international travel. *Zemel v. Rusk* (1965) 381 U.S. 1, held that such orders were valid and constitutional.

Therefore, the freedom to travel abroad is a recognized freedom but it may be limited for governmental purposes and laws limiting that right are valid, unless the limitations are wholly irrational. *Zemel* obviously felt that the menace of Communism, the safety of Americans in Cuba, and the avoidance of international incidents with nations declared to be unfriendly were more than enough reasons to infringe on the right to travel to another country.

5. Do I have a "right" to own a passport?

The case of *Kent v. Dulles* (1958) 357 U.S. 116, held that a passport cannot be denied because of the political beliefs or associations of the applicant. The *Kent* case, in a 5-4 decision, reversed the State Department's denial of a passport to artist Rockwell Kent, who refused to submit an affidavit disclaiming any affiliation with Communist groups.   Therefore, both Communists and Republicans may apply for a passport and unwarranted restrictions cannot be justified, such as making the applicant give up organization membership — freedom of association is itself a constitutional right.

6. How do I obtain a passport?

We know from the *Kent* case that any adult (whose liberty is not otherwise limited) may acquire a passport by proper application to the State Department. Applications may be found in your post office and they ask for statistical information concerning your proof of birth, and photos, as well as an application fee.

Be aware that restrictions and revocations may occur even though they undeniably curtail your "rights" involving travel. The ex-CIA agent, Philip Agee, began a campaign in Europe during the 1970s to expose CIA officers and agents who were working abroad and, accordingly, revealed identities and other classified information. Feeling that his activities were prejudicial to the United States, the Secretary of State revoked Agee's passport. In *Haig v. Agee* (1981) 101 S. Ct. 2766, it was held that the revocation was permissible and did not violate Agee's constitutional rights. That case answered your questions about travel rights by making it plain that the *freedom* to travel internationally must be distinguished from the *right* to travel within the United States.

7. **Could I relocate abroad and have my welfare or Social Security benefits sent to me?**

It would be difficult under a new identity and your question makes it sound like you are trying to have your cake and eat it too — you would like to leave but you would like to retain the benefits of your current situation.

Realize that you would have to notify the agency giving you benefits and possibly request a new payee name, thereby leaving a paper trail about your relocation — information that could be discovered by court order or other methods.

As for permission from the agency paying you benefits, you may find that parts of certain laws forbid the paying of benefits for any month that the recipient spends entirely outside of the U.S. Just such a rule was challenged in the U.S. Supreme Court in *Califano v. Aznavorian* (1978) 439 U.S. 170, and the rule was held to be valid. Therefore, you are free to travel but certain government benefits may be withdrawn during and shortly after an extended absence from the United States.

On the other hand, other benefits — such as private retirement funds, veteran disability payments, and social security payments — are payable to addresses outside of the U.S., but not likely to a new identity without a legal name change and the resulting paper trail linking your new identity with your old identity.

8. **Is it possible to travel to any foreign country without a passport?**

Entry to Canada and Mexico is still possible on a birth certificate, the Canadian border being largely unguarded and the Mexican authorities allowing the passage of Americans who declare tourism for a short period as their reason for visiting.

9. **What foreign country would be the best to relocate to? What foreign countries currently allow the immigration of Americans?**

As far as what is "best" for you, only you can answer that question, as it involves personal preferences, financial resources, and immigration availability.

Personal preferences involve taking stock of your previous travel and life experiences, foreign language skills, your own ethnic background and relatives in foreign countries.

Limits on financial resources are probably the greatest obstacle to relocation within another country. If you had huge sums of money, you might realize a very comfortable and civilized stay in the south of France — much like many deposed leaders of state who now live there. With fewer resources, the only inexpensive non-Soviet European nations are Ireland, Portugal, and Greece. A step cheaper are the emerging eastern-European countries, but you would undoubtedly find a poorer standard of living and almost no chance of finding work. Cheaper still are the somewhat unstable, "third world" nations of Asia, Africa, and South America. Take stock of what you can afford and what hardships you are willing to put up with.

Immigration ability is also of major concern because while almost every nation will let you visit, very few will let you stay indefinitely without having baskets of money. Many major U.S. cities have offices which represent foreign nations and which are referred to as "consulates." Phone calls to the consulates of different nations will give you entry requirements, application procedures, background investigations, and the waiting periods which are appropriate.

10. **Is it possible to obtain a passport under a new identity?**

It is possible although you would be providing false information to the State Department and therefore in violation of the law. See the Case History after Chapter Ten for a discussion of an escaped felon who travelled from Texas to Africa and back.

Case History:
John, The Man With Three Ex-Wives

John came back to the States after being wounded in the Korean War and got married. A couple of decades later, all he had left was his veteran's disability pension, while three ex-wives and bill collectors were hounding him. "I had to get the hell away from them — just *had* to get away," said John.

I met John in Sydney, Australia, where he was doing "a little business" and "coming out of hiding for awhile." He informed me he had his V.A. checks sent to Hawaii where a friend deposited them in an account set up under a pseudonym. John had been living in the Philippines and his bank there let him transfer from the Hawaiian account and everything had gone swimmingly for years.

"I had a limited income and I thought about where it would go the farthest, so I made a choice between Mexico, Central America, and the Philippines," said John. "The Philippines is a place where they like Americans and where the Yankee dollar goes a long way. I have a good house and a maid for about $150 U.S. per month. Now that I'm used to the food, the place is home."

I asked John about the heat and he said that because the Philippines were volcanic, there were huge mountains. "A little elevation and it's quite cool again," John said. "Besides, once a year I come to Australia as a tourist and get to see civilization again."

John still uses his real name in the Philippines because he travels on an American passport in that name. He also told me that his residence in the South Pacific was not forever, so a name change would be just a hassle. "I'll go back to the States someday," said John. "I just want those damn wives to grow older and remarry." His only trail cover was the deposit of his V.A. check in the Hawaiian account. "That's another good thing about the Philippines. They'll work with you. A few bucks and you can get anything there."

CHAPTER NINE: FAKING DEATH

1. Presumptions Upon Disappearance
2. Presumption of Death
3. Distribution of Estate Upon Presumption of Death
4. Circumstantial Evidence of Death
5. Faking Death

1. **If I disappear, what will people presume?**

They will presume you are missing, of course. In California, if you own property and are missing for ninety days, friends or relatives can petition by way of a method described in the Probate Code to have a trustee take charge of your property.

The trustee would have duties and responsibilities to take care of the property by collecting income, paying bills, and may even be granted the power to mortgage or sell your property. If the missing person returns, the trustee must account for the funds that have come in and gone out.

2. **What if I stay missing? Will they presume I'm dead?**

In California, when a person is missing for over seven years, an attempt may be made to administer the missing person's estate by invoking the presumption of death from seven years' absence found in the California Evidence Code. Other states have similar presumptions.

In that situation, your estate would not be merely cared for by a trustee but would be settled and divided among your heirs. The Order of Distribution would be accompanied by an Order that you were presumed dead.

Usually some showing must be made of search and inquiry to locate the missing person before the presumption will arise. However, there are no fixed steps of search and each disappearance would create a different type of necessary search. For example, a person swept away by a fast-moving river would promote a search that would be different from a person who did not come back to work after his lunch break.

3. **How will my estate be distributed if I don't have a will?**

Dying without a will is described as *intestacy* and each state has statutory provisions that describe how your estate would be settled in that situation. Typically, it would go first to an existing spouse, then to children or parents, then to siblings.

California's missing persons statute creates a distinct procedure for the final distribution of the property of a person missing for the requisite period. The legality and constitutionality of that type of legislation has been upheld in *Sevier v. Bank of America* (1950) 101 CA2d 184.

4. May death be presumed in other ways?

Yes, death may be presumed by circumstantial evidence, or the circumstances under which you disappeared and which tend to indicate death. If you board a plane and the plane crashes into the bay, although your body cannot be found you may be presumed dead after an appropriate search.

In *Estate of Christin* (1933) 128 CA 625 the court considered the circumstances of the missing person's health. In that case, the husband escaped from an insane asylum and was not heard from for over seven years. His wife did not hear from him and died five years after his escape. It was held that evidence of the husband's serious illness justified the conclusion that he predeceased his wife. In other words, the circumstantial evidence led to a presumption of death before seven years had passed.

In *People v. Niccoli* (1951) 102 CA2d 814 there was an argument over whether or not Mr. Niccoli's bondsman had to forfeit bail. The circumstances were that Mr. Niccoli disappeared, leaving his car near an airport, and that an intensive search failed to locate him. It was held that where a motive exists as a reason for disappearance, the presumption of life continued for seven years. There the evidence also showed that Mr. Niccoli was penniless, that he had been indicted, that he had removed labels from his clothing and changed the license plates on his car, and that he was a member of a group in disrepute. All of the evidence showed a good reason for flight. Accordingly, the court upheld the order which made the bondsman forfeit the bail.

5.   **What if I notified the police that a person fell in the river and was swept away? I could leave some of my items of property on the bank of the river and the police would infer my death.**

Be aware that the California Penal Code, and the laws of most other states, make presenting a false claim to a governmental agency a felony.

The arrangement of your "items" may be preparing false evidence, a crime which is also a felony, in that it is preparing evidence which may be used or produced for a fraudulent purpose (your "death") in an action to declare you deceased.

Further, if you have any ideas that you would fake your death and have insurance proceeds paid to a beneficiary, the California Insurance Code, and similar statutes in most other states, establish the felony of fraudulent insurance claims.

All of these crimes are actively prosecuted when the fraud is discovered. Therefore, I advise you not to participate in any activity which would carry out this daydream of your apparent death. I can understand the moment of drama when you "reappeared" years later, or when you read your own obituary with amusement, but those little dramas would only happen after you have committed frauds upon people and government — frauds which would amount to serious crimes. Don't do it.

Case History:
Andre, The Thief

The one and only time I had dealings with the evidentiary presumption of death involved Andre, a European immigrant who went back to his country of birth as often as his finances would allow. He would always return to San Francisco with small, European antiques which he would peddle to the dealers of antiques and purveyors of objets d'art. One year, Andre made the rounds with several Russian icons and made a small fortune; the next year, he had fragments of marble statuary — small stone hands and faces — which he sold only with difficulty.

One year, Andre went to Europe and did not return. His aunt died a few years later and, as the settlement of her estate neared, the relatives wondered what to do with Andre's share. Some relatives said Andre's inheritance should be held in trust. Other relatives had made inquiries in Europe and, as not a trace of Andre could be found, they felt he could be declared dead and his inheritance divided among the remaining heirs. One relative asked me to begin the Probate Code petition which would declare Andre's death.

The next month, after the filing of the petition but prior to the court hearing at which time evidence of disappearance and circumstances of death would be heard, Andre arrived in San Francisco — still alive. Our hearing was taken off calendar and I was deprived of the experience of having someone declared dead.

It seems that Andre was bringing stolen European antiques to America — articles small enough to carry through customs on his person. While I was never in direct contact with Andre, I was given the impression from a relative that Andre was "obtaining" the antiques from private collections, churches, and even museums by theft. Andre's disappearance without a trace was due to his incarceration for a number of years for the stealing and attempted transportation of government-protected antiques. His luck returned, however, as his release was just timely enough for him to claim his share of the inheritance.

CHAPTER TEN:
CHANCES OF SUCCESS

1. What are my chances of success with a new identity?

Succeeding at what? This may be the time to ask yourself why you would want to relocate. List your goals and, if those goals can be met, your relocation may be a success.

If you are considering relocation because your girl-friend(s) is/are unbearable, you may relocate from Idaho only to find the women on the other side of the country in Alabama are just as difficult. If that's the case, you might realize that the trouble is (at least partly) *you*. You have imported the "problem" with you and no amount of relocation will fix it until you look inward and make adjustments in your own character.

If you are considering relocation because an old friend or lover is bothering, or even stalking you, then success will be achieved by having a period of time go by without contact with that individual. After you have lived a year under a new identity and without contact from him or her, you can think in terms of success.

Therefore, plan a relocation the way you would plan the repair of an engine — an orderly, step-by-step process with certain goals in mind. Make a list or otherwise state your goals. Now ask yourself if those goals are achievable through a relocation.

2. What are common ways to screw up?

By repeating the same mistakes there that you made here.

Are you leaving because your so-called "friends" have deserted you or, on the other hand, want to beat you up? The best way to avoid that happening again at your relocation venue is to pick good friends and be a good friend in return. That, of course, involves values and behavior that you may or may not be able to rely on having.

Every so often, there is a human interest story about an escaped prisoner who is returned to custody after being free for several years. Why was that missing individual undiscovered for so long? Because he or she led a productive, low-key life and avoided contact with the justice system. In short, the missing person stopped making the mistakes that got him or her noticed and into trouble in the first place.

3. What can I do now that I've left and relocated?

Double-check to see that your trail has been covered. I've hounded you about changing habits and routines, as well as letting go of items of personal property that can identify you.

Next, try to stop any paper trail to you by avoiding the use of telltale phones or bank accounts. Do not send letters to old friends.

Do not contact old friends in any other way, including surprise visits. Do not engage in any behavior which will bring you into suspicion or cause contact with the justice system.

Finally, do not show this book to anyone and, now that you have read it, destroy it as soon as possible.

Case History:
Bill Allen, Escaped Convict

Traveling in a car with four other black men in Nashville on January 16, 1968, a companion of Bill Allen's became involved in a shootout with police and two officers were killed. Allen left Nashville and became the object of a huge FBI search. Pictures were circulated and all of Allen's friends and relatives were questioned. Through that and other police work, Allen was taken into custody and returned to Tennessee. Because of the historical and geographical setting, there was an emotional charge to the trial which commenced just after Thanksgiving, 1968, and which resulted in a sentence for Allen of ninety-nine years.

On May 11, 1974, after over six years in custody, Bill Allen changed into civilian clothes on a visiting day and went to the prison's picnic grounds. He mingled with visitors and literally walked out of prison, then caught a ride to Georgia.

As described in *On The Run*, a book by Al Browning, Allen settled into a normal life, obtaining a job, making friends with a reliable woman, and being known only by a new identity. He studied business opportunities, considered emigrating to Africa, and eventually relocated to Texas. Interstate flight after a prison escape is a federal offense that activates FBI jurisdiction and the federal agents were, indeed, looking for Allen.

Bill Allen, however, remained inconspicuous and free — by 1984 a married businessman with children, tending to a trading company that he founded, and traveling to and from Nigeria on an American passport to investigate business opportunities. In 1992, a Department of Motor Vehicles clerk alerted authorities on a suspicion, ending his eighteen years on the run.

YOU WILL ALSO WANT TO READ:

☐ **61115 REBORN IN THE U.S.A. Personal Privacy through a New Identity,** *Second Edition, by Trent Sands.* A complete guide to building a new identity in the United States from the ground up. Covers birth certificates, Social Security card, drivers license, passport, credit cards, and much more. Learn how to thoroughly document your new identity without revealing any information about your former life. *1991, 5½ x 8½, 121 pp, soft cover.* **$14.95.**

☐ **61139 METHODS OF DISGUISE, 2nd Edition,** *by John Sample. Newly revised and expanded.* Need a new look to go with your new I.D.? Everything from "quick change" methods to long-term permanent disguises are covered in illustrated detail. Disguise yourself so completely even old friends won't recognize you! *1993, 5½ x 8½, 264 pp, illustrated, soft cover.* **$14.95.**

☐ **61127 REBORN OVERSEAS, Identity Building in Europe, Australia, and New Zealand,** *by Trent Sands.* The formation of the European Common Market has created a paper-tripping paradise. With an identity in any one nation, you can live, work and travel in all twelve. This book shows how to get all the documents necessary to build a complete paper identity without leaving the United States. *1991, 5½ x 8½, 110 pp, illustrated, soft cover.* **$14.95.**

☐ **61111 COUNTERFEIT I.D. MADE EASY,** *by Jack Luger.* A complete guide to making your own I.D.! Using common tools and readily-available materials, you can make photo ID cards, drivers licenses, birth certificates, and much more. *Sold for informational purposes. 1990, 5½ x 8½, 131 pp, illustrated, soft cover.* **$9.95.**

And much more! We offer the very finest in controversial and unusual books— please turn to our catalog advertisement on the next page. Our catalog is free with any book ordered above.

··

Loompanics Unlimited
PO Box 1197
Port Townsend, WA 98368
(206) 385-2230

SCRM94

Please send me the books I have checked above. I have enclosed $_____ which includes $4.00 for shipping and handling of 1 to 3 books, $6.00 for 4 or more. (Washington residents include 7.9% sales tax.)

Name_____

Address _____

City _____

State/Zip_____

Now accepting Visa and MasterCard.